In Search of Lost Birds

In Search of Lost Birds

Poems by

Ellen Rowland

Cover design by Shay Culligan
Cover image by Birger Strahl
Author photo by Sunny Rowland

ISBN: 979-8-90146-717-6

Kelsay Books
502 South 1040 East, A-119
American Fork, Utah 84003
Kelsaybooks.com

Each poem in this collection is an homage to
another poet—living or ancestral—whose words
have inspired, surprised, lifted, comforted,
and taught me how to be a better poet.
This book is dedicated to them.

May the conversation continue.

Acknowledgments

Many thanks to the editors of the following journals, anthologies, or collections in which these poems first appeared:

Autumn Sky Poetry Daily: “Making Room”

Lines of Communication Anthology (The Wee Sparrow Poetry Press): “In the Clover Patch—The Poet at Ten”

No Small Thing (Fernwood Press, 2023): “Transformation”

One Art: a Journal of Poetry: “Endangered Pleasure”

Sheila Na Gig: “Lacrimal Gland”

My deep gratitude to poets Jen Feroze and Patrick Ramsay for their time, consideration, and generosity in offering kind and thoughtful words of praise for this collection, and to James Crews for his continued support and encouragement of my work. This book would not be possible without the ever-growing community of poets who nourish and enlighten me. Thank you for sharing your brave words.

Contents

Every poem has ancestors.

—Joy Harjo

Lacrimal Gland

After William Stafford

Sometimes, when I'm lying on my side
reading poetry in bed, I feel a single tear
leave the corner of my eye and slide down
my cheek onto the pillow. Because there is
no obvious emotion attached to the tear,
I used to think it was merely a sign of fatigue
or eye strain, a plea to close the book and sleep.
But more and more, I wonder if this isn't a wholly
human reaction to someone who has chiseled
diamonds with a pen, wrapped their hard story
in rosemary and lavender, performed open-heart
surgery, handed you the heart still beating and said,
Here, take it, it's yours.

Music

After Christian Wiman

Lullaby, most gentle word—
like the sway of the womb,
pulse of steady heart
heard underwater,
it's fusion of *lull* and *by.*

Or *song,* perhaps—so lovely
on the tongue, so close to *slung*
or *sung,* how the lips obey
lungs as *ess* passes softly through
rest, rest.

How the mouth forms
the shape of itself, presses warmth
to tender forehead, balled fist, soft belly,
as voice becomes a night sky
in which to float.

In the Clover Patch—The Poet at Ten

After Jane Kenyon

She searches cross-legged for the one
with four leaves, four hearts joined.
The rare one that will bring her luck. A breeze,
light, warm and slightly annoying,
brings whisps of hair before her eyes

but does not, could not, stop her steady combing.

She ties the two sides of the curtain
into a knot at the back of her head
never taking her eyes off the impression
of where her fingers last were.

The humming field in full sun, that small island
in the circular driveway, is so vast and full of possibility,
that she parts her world in two—
One side, explored. The other, waiting.

When All Is Cold

After Alix Klingenberg

Turn toward the things that comfort you—
the wick you light each morning
as ritual with coffee and ink, small shadow
of morning moth, curious and circling.
The thinned cardigan that smells
of dry-cleaning, rain, and your father
deep in the weave. Both strange
and familiar arms, asked for too often
and kept too long because you had
no idea how much you'd missed
the simple pull of heart on heart,
right cheek to right cheek, the kind
of embrace that makes you sigh
all the way back to a childhood of free
holding, given without asking. A knee
to lay your head on in church, light lips
pressed to your forehead before sleep.
A warm towel held out to welcome you
from a bath gone cold. The rough and tender
ruffling of wet hair. Your mother's voice,
muffled, imagined.

Two Golden Shovels

After José A. Alcántara

Beyond

Hummingbirds
arrive
beating
their small delicate hearts, thrill notes of their
dawn silent through glass. I am invisible
to them, sipping coffee, testing my own wings
stiff from sleep, penning words beyond
what I intended and that no one will read. The
light breaks in pinks and salmons, a window.

Transformation

My
wet wings
spread, tracing
infinity.
I hardly miss my
brutish legs, once dull throat.
Mouth of this joyful turning
now a beak of song, longing to
spill forth like a belch of bright rubies.

I Wish I Could Sing

A cento composed of lines from Mary Oliver

Every day I see or hear something
that kills me with delight.
The field and the sparrow singing
at the edge of the woods, the underwings
as sunlight flushes into feathers.

Every year I gather handfuls of blossoms
and eat their mealiness. I am watching
the lilies bow to each other. Sad, isn't it,
that all they can kiss is the air? I know now
what they want is to touch each other.

When I am alone, I can become invisible
in the dark hug of time. I think about
what it is that music is trying to say.
My heart dresses in black and dances.
The spirit likes to dress up like this.

At the First Drop of Rain

After Stanley Kunitz

every cell and pore opens,
every follicle and ventricle
expands to receive.
What hand pulls it down
with such insistence? Desire.
Desire to be known, deep loam,
dormant vine, parched clay,
beaks and throats and gills
all bare themselves to the soak
as if to say, *touch me, remind me*
who I am. It's been so long
since you've asked me to dance.

You

After Rainer Maria Rilke

I close my eyes and there You are,
the you that defies description
no matter how hard I may try.
The tallest pine branch
that sways to meet the kestrel's talons.
The first seed on the spiral of a sunflower
making room for its future self.
The space behind the breast plate
that begins an inhale before the mind
can even think of air. Despair
softening into home and nest,
a space that is as wide and timeless
as the mystery of sorrow and song.
I imagine my soul is the sunflower,
is the pine tree, is the kestrel, is the breath.
Then the knowing comes and settles in
like the cold around a bonfire.

Sunflower

After Angelina Weld Grimké

Tell me, is there anything lovelier,
anything more reassuring
than the bright yellow of a sunflower
and the gentle green of its crown?

Is not each bold head a smiling nod to life?
Is not each lush leaf and proud stalk
a defiance of death, born into its own hushed
heaven every morning?

For the Twig, the Round Moon

After Naomi Shihab Nye

I am thankful for the cold dry twig
attached to its last gold leaf,
lifelines intact, one small hole I hold
to my eye like a monocle.
I am thankful for that round pigeon
of a moon, that best nightlight
for a porch gazer like me
wrapped in a shawl
throwing stones at the neon streetlight,
willing to pay the fine
just to see the salt the gods scattered
for anyone who cares to adore.

I'd rather be influenced

After Patrick Ramsay

to let my hair go gray, to embrace the crow's feet
at the corners of my eyes, those deep, dancing
heel marks of a lifetime of laughter and worry.
I don't want to be offered more goods I don't need.
I'd rather be tempted to fall in love
with what I already have—the last zucchini
in the garden, the perfect non-stick pan,
sauteed goodness coated with herbs most would consider
weeds, loved and plucked and lingering on fingertips,
on chipped porcelain plates, the spice-stained palate.
I want an algorithm that worships my hips,
wide and wonderful and soft, having walked
and climbed and swayed their way to this moment.
I won't click on your ad for the perfect diet. Give me
full cream and salted butter, strong black coffee,
tangy lemon bars dusted with powdered sugar.
My bare feet carried me from one end of the beach
to the other this morning. The light glimmered
off lapping waves that licked my ankles with cold,
blue tongues. You had to be there.

The Herd

After Ellen Bass

My social media feed is cluttered with women
in sports bras doing squats against the living room wall,
claiming six pack abs at sixty-five.
I am taunted daily by magical menopause powders
proffered by a company called "Happy Mammoth,"
as though all women over 50 must be massive,
lumbering, quickly approaching extinction—and celebrating.
I feel woolly and defeated, distracted, and distended.
To the leotarded and the flat-bellied, I say, good for you!
Your cholesterol levels must be stellar.
But just to balance the scales, I proclaim to the lusty lovers
of occasional triple-cream cheese—*Bless butter! Bless brie!*
Celebrate their oozy union wrapped in puff pastry and robed
in apricot jam. Praise the hills, valleys, and dips of hips
and bosom, the simple state of titillated taste buds.
May pleasure continue to roam the cold tundra,
trembling the earth in search of its herd.

Cake Credo

After Donna Hilbert

I believe in screenless, scroll-free Sundays,
time to linger-flip the pages of cookbooks
searching for a recipe to use up an abundance
of raspberries from a rain-inspired harvest.

I believe in the art of a chocolate tart, bedding the sweet,
red-ripe buttons between layers of dark buttered batter
while church bells ring in the village and I pause
to listen to their pealing, offer up a whispered *thank you*
and kiss the fluted cake pan.

I believe in the slow bake, oven at eye level, the tick
of the spring-load timer as I sit with scented alchemy,
the boiling pot, the rising roil, which, bless the old wives,
does indeed come to quiver under my watchful gaze.

I believe in loose leaf tea steeped in a floating ball
left to brew as I slice the confection and call my love
to the altar of the cake stand, where we are silent
with simple awe at what we are about to eat.

And I believe that the fingertip, swiped and licked,
is a fine way to clean a white plate. This cake, this man,
this savored, sugared moment may be all I need in life
and all I ask of heaven.

Endangered Pleasure

After James Crews

Add this to my list of small ecstasies:
the way honey creams together
with butter on freshly baked bread,
the innocence of its warm alchemy
as churn, as rise, as breaking down
of simple sugar. I swear I can taste
the tantra of the hive, the tending to
of queen by drone, the dripping cone,
workers' legs impossibly laden with
thick pollen, deposited and darned.
This, from the buttercups and purslanes
most would have condemned to the curb
as bothersome weed. This from the common
dandelions we left to riot just for the bees.
An entire patch of golden suns now radiating
as endangered pleasure on my tongue.

Do I Dare?

After T.S. Eliot

Do I dare eat a peach
in the chilly ides of fall?
Do I twist apart its mottled cheeks
and hope I might recall

the bliss of summers tender
or the curve of turquoise bowl,
cicadas in their splendor
keeping time to limbs in fold?

Do we dare share this peach?
there's nothing left to taste:
the flesh, the salt, the skin, the beach,
were all consumed in haste.

This Is How It Happened

After Rita Dove

After the wind, this air
dove-grey and still,
then day at the window,
late yellow and crisp.
A rust-colored finch
dislodges the last
sycamore leaf.
Bird flies away—sky
leaf wends its way—earth
and in between
silk sheets become flannel.

Lockets

A cento composed of lines from various authors

Bowl daylight fell through
this ragged January,
as if a long sleep had ended.
What song to sing down an empty road?
I have to commit to something in this life.
Not sleep, not a lover,
but the smell of ferns and understory after rain.
I simply put my arms around a tall oak.
There is no swaying, her trunk
a melody of secret rings, like an ancestor.
See how everything gathers the light
inside itself, like lockets?

For Today

After Jane Hirshfield

a small sparrow sings
as the streets flush with ashes
a mother dances
for the ones they didn't take
and the copper bowls balance

In Search of Lost Birds

After Mahmoud Darwish

Where have all the birds gone
in Gaza? Are they still around
seeking perch, crumb, thread?
Do trees still stand or do mothers
nest in walls of rubble? Are there
worms, grubs, snails? Or is the soil
too soaked with blood, layered
with ash and littered lives?
At home, a robin sings
despite the headlines,
like she has a promise to keep
with song and light and nothing
can stop her. I can't imagine
the pierce of bird song there
through so much death, sad air.
What music could survive
when no one is listening?

One Word Prayer

After Mary Katherine Creel

Because the world is in need of mercy,
I find myself before the sun has risen
whispering the word *help*
to what feels like a heaven stretched thin.

Help, I say again, small one word prayer
repeats itself, a makeshift mantra:
help, help, help
Who am I pleading with, I wonder,

in this house of silence? Who alone
can hold the weight of this frayed world?
and more and more and more gone.
Help, I offer to the cool morning air,

hands joined, head bent to the beast of it
and I stay there, gathering them all
into the space between my palms.
Light arrives so slowly these days.

Graft

After Michael Kleber-Diggs

Can't you feel it?
We are reaching for each other all the time,
above and below ground. Listen.
Someone is thundering toward you
right this moment with oxygen, nutrients,
a branch, a bough, a bird
in shock, but recovering. Take
what is given and offer in kind.
Proffer the crow's shiny trinket,
the snail's warm chamber,
your bruiseless fruit, your fondest sweater,
all the scars of your heart.
This is our nature,
to graft each other's wounds,
planted here as we are
in all kinds of skin.

Making Room

After Heather Swan

Come, sit with me, stranger.
I promise I won't ask what you do
or where you stand
or what side you're on
because this bench is sturdy,
which is to say
it can hold the two of us—
our barbaric selves
our buried twinship
our tired, heavy bones.
I'll make room for you,
which is to say
I'll move my bag
full of fear and anger,
brush off the fragile leaves
that once felt like death
but now seem to be teachers.
They've fallen
in kinship with the wind,
which is to say torn
which is to say displaced
which is to say cradled.
Look, our shadowed silhouettes
are leaning into each other,
a kind of trust we aren't ready
to imagine.

Afternoon

After Jane Kenyon

It's quiet here.
Your absence is a presence,
a thin white curtain
that billows though there's no breeze
and settles just as I rise.

Fist-Heart Turned Peony

After Diana Whitney

Because she was no bigger than a small fig
when she unexpectedly slipped from my womb,
you would think she takes up the same amount
of space in my heart. The heart, they say, being
the size of a closed fist, so much smaller than
one would think. But how elastic we are in love,
how shapeless in grief. She, and others I have lost
over the years—friends, mother, father, loves—
occupy all of me. When the fist opens, splaying
its delicate fingers, their souls find hiding places:
hip joint, shoulder blade, sacrum, tear ducts,
pit of stomach, back of throat. They flood me
with ache before returning to my fist-heart,
now a pink-flushed peony, allowing me to
love them all over again to the pulse of
remember remember remember.

It’s a Lot to Ask

After Linda Hogan

It’s a lot to ask
of the wintering woods—
of skink, of whipsnake,
of mouse-earred bat,
of the pair of lesser kestrels
inseparable as they glide and perch.
I’ve been pleading lately, too,
with ancient plane and pine:
Can you unharm me?
I’m on my knees.
No one says I’m selfish.
No one says a word.

What the Soil Knows

After Elizabeth Willis

The young tree that dies is not a failure.
The Braeburn red and the Bosc pear did their best
in the June heat that came early.

The first sign of rot is softness. The way the skin loosens
in places that are no longer touched, no longer cared for.
All life is an endless cycle of attention. Inattention.

That was the day I noticed the wood worm.
That was the day I turned 60.

Celebrations are guestless and calm. Years don't feel thread-like.
Still thirty in my mind, but my breasts are no longer firm and pink-flushed.
My trunk is not pear-like. So much left to be thankful for. We drink cider.

This was not a birth. It was not a death. Not the same grief.
A different becoming.

Sixty years, too many days to count. A life is not to be calculated. We loved
with no clock. We pulled apart and felt our way back.

Death is what we ignored until the tree bent at the waste. This is what we saw
when we were looking. We know there is life and not life. But it was spring
and then it was a season we didn't recognize.

This is how we surrender.
This is what the soil knows.

Archeology

After Babette Deutsch

The winter-plucked ground has frosted overnight,
each blade of wheatgrass and patch of clay-cracked
soil robed in a slick, delicate glaze. The soil,
once solid, now has the aspect of burnt sugar
crème brûlée. The tip of my garden boot tests
its fragile sheath and it cracks into a thousand
glimmering ice hairs, tiny burgs breaking
to reveal a bright green leaf of vetch vine
and the tiniest purple petals below, tricked
into birth by a rogue week of warmth.
Frost and bloom should never meet.
We know this. And yet, here we are
pushing, digging, exposing—
insisting on beauty.

On a Winter Morning

After Ted Kooser

One small blue flame rings the kettle's whisper.
A well-worn teapot holds dried remnants
of summer's generous patch, gathered
and tied with string, strung from the rafters,
stored in rubber-lipped jars. A tip of honey,
a single clove in a chipped china cup.
A pitted silver spoon—cold to the touch—
sings against the sides, hums through still cream
again and again, until the light begins to change
from oat, to wheat, to golden flax. Farmhouse,
field and lover all come awake with it.

Shaping a Soft Place

After James Crews

We bring them in cages at dusk,
open the metal grid hatch to the hen house
and transfer the young brood to their new home.
At dawn, the rooster crows us awake
in comical predictability and we rush to them
like children on Christmas morning.
The pullets have gathered the wood shavings
into a soft pile, pushing the sides up
like dough in a pie tin, leaving the impression
of body as home. A white feather floats.

Once, dazed and discovering my new room
in an empty home in an unfamiliar town, I unpacked
favorite books and stacked them carefully
on freshly painted shelves, softening the echo.
Arranged chipped teacups the size of acorn hats
next to the Spanish doll in red flamenco dress.
Unfurled the crimson flower in her hair,
petal by petal, as my mother pulled
a clean sheet from a box, snapped it
into the air and let it fall.

Such Love If You Let It

After Ross Gay

When your husband passes by you
as you're doing dishes at the sink,
the thing you love the least,
and says, *come see this*
his thumb on the pulse point of your wrist
as he leads you outside
to show you the perfect pale blue egg,
the very first one the Chilean Araucana
has laid. When he says, *go ahead*
and the still-warm orb cradles perfectly
in your palm, and he asks, *should I*
make us more coffee? And you lead him back,
rinse two cups, two teaspoons, put your hands
over your ears as the coffee grinder whirs
the scent of all your mornings and you say,
What? Did you say something?
and you both laugh.

Dinner

After Jane Kenyon

We sit across from each other
at the worn wooden table, two lit candles
between us, place holders perhaps
for the nest, empty now for many months.
The ritual of low lights and the incense
of a quiche, clear stems tilting to toast our day.
Rows of small potatoes planted and put to bed
for a mid-summer harvest when
we'll find them again, utterly changed.
Suddenly, I understand we are happy.
Before we begin, you rise and close
the curtains. They meet perfectly
like the lids of a cardboard box
sealing in something fragile.

Wider Than That

A cento composed of lines from Mary Oliver

My life with its poems and its music
is to lie down by a slow river
and stare at the light in the trees—
to learn something by being nothing.

The sky is blue, or the rain falls
with its spill of pearl, this dazzling darkness
coming down the mountain.
Each of us wears a shadow.

The black smocked crickets,
and the dragonflies, if they happen
to be out late over the ponds, don't
even know they have wings.

So listen to them and watch them singing
as they fly, just beyond your shoulder,
a beautiful hurricane of light,
yawning, gathering.

Lean your arms on the sill
and accept the miracle.
It will nuzzle your face, cold-nosed
like a small white wolf.

Each time I finish a poem,

After Jen Feroze

I'm afraid I'll never write anything again.
Afraid there will be no more beauty. The sky
will wash out unnoticed, the sun will lose its yoke
rise, its white linen ascension, its mandarin setting.
I'm afraid my eyes won't catch the shimmer of opal
light off the oil slicked sea. Afraid the fish won't
swim past my gaze, fixed and searching too hard.
Afraid I won't smell the fig sap oozing from the burning
log in the woodstove I won't be warmed by. Afraid
my lips will no longer purse at the burst of kaffir lime
or the peppery cardamon pod in the bowl of red dal.
Afraid I will never again hum to leaf arias, never long
to be a bird, never fall in love with what I have not heard.
Not because I have died, but because I don't yet trust
that I will be born again into wonder—the crisp white
sheet flapping on the line, *the sudden flash of a kingfisher*
moving out of my periphery and into full view.

How You Know

For and after James Crews

You will know
when the perfect poem has found you
at the exact moment you need it
when the words land as though
they were written just for you—
in joy or sorrow or pain. When the hummingbird,
or the zested orange, or a mother's fragile hand
becomes so real, you can see it, smell it, hold it.
As though the poet saw into your heart,
and as they lifted their pen, what fell to paper
was not just thoughts put down in ink,
but a red thread of knowing tethered
between you across oceans and time zones.
And you feel safe and seen and understood.
And you say to yourself, "This one."
"This one is my favorite."

Credits and Notes

"Lacrimal Gland" borrows a line from "The Gift" by William Stafford from *My Name is William Tell* (Confluence Press, 1992).

"Music" is inspired by "Prelude in Grey Major" by Christian Wiman, *The New Yorker* online, December 2024.

"In the Clover Patch—The Poet at Ten" is inspired by "In the Grove: The Poet at Ten" by Jane Kenyon from *The Best Poems of Jane Kenyon* (Greywolf Press, 2020).

"When All Is Cold" is inspired by the poem of the same title by Alix Klingenberg from *Quietly Wild* (Mandela Earth, 2025).

"Beyond" and "Transformation" are Golden Shovels based on lines in stanzas 1 and 2 from "Archilochus Colubris" by José A. Alcántara from *The Bitten World* (Tebot Bach, 2021).

"I Wish I Could Sing" is a cento poem composed of lines by Mary Oliver. All poems from *Devotions* (Penguin Press, 2017). Line credits as follows:

Title: "The Pond"
Lines 1, 2: "Mindful"
Lines 3, 4: "Blueberries"
Lines 4, 5: "The Vultures Wings"
Lines 6, 7: "Honey Locust"
Lines 7, 8: "The Pond"
Lines 8, 9 : "I Know Someone"
Lines 9, 10: "The Pond"
Lines 11, 12: "How I go to the Woods," "Poem"

Line 12, 13: "Drifting"
Line 14: "After Reading Lucretius, I go to the Pond"
Line 15: "Poem"

"At the First Drop of Rain" is inspired by "Touch Me" by Stanley Kunitz from *Passing Through: The Later Poems, New and Selected* (W.W. Norton, 1995).

"You" is inspired by "Ich liebe meines Wesens Dunkelstunden" I,5 by Rainer Maria Rilke from *Rilke's Book of Hours: Love Poems to God,* translated by Anita Barrows and Joanna Macy (Riverhead Books, 1996).

"Sunflower" is inspired by "Greenness" by Angelina Weld Grimké from *Caroling Dusk: An Anthology of Verse by Negro Poets* (Harper and Row, 1927).

"For the Twig, the Round Moon" is inspired by a phrase in "Different Ways to Pray" by Naomi Shihab Nye from *Words Under the Words: Selected Poems* (Far Corner Books, 1995).

"I'd rather be influenced" is inspired by a poem of the same title by Patrick Ramsay originally published online at *Gwarlingo,* July, 2022.

"The Herd" is inspired by "Ode to Fat" by Ellen Bass from *Indigo* (Copper Canyon Press, 2020).

"Cake Credo" is inspired by a line from "Credo" by Donna Hilbert from *The Green Season,* 2nd edition (World Parade Books, 2012).

“Endangered Pleasure” is inspired by and borrows the first line of “Love What Comes” by James Crews published online in *Cultural Daily,* August, 2023.

“Do I Dare?” is inspired by “The Love Song of J. Alfred Prufrock” by T.S. Eliot, first published in *Poetry: A Magazine of Verse,* June 1915.

“This Is How It Happened” is inspired by a line from “Persephone in Hell, VI” by Rita Dove from *Mother Love* (W.W. Norton & Company, 1995).

“Lockets” is a cento composed of lines borrowed from various poems from the anthology *The Wonder of Small Things: Poems of Peace and Renewal,* edited by James Crews (Storey Publishing, 2023). Line credits as follows:

Line 1: Dorianne Laux, “My Mother’s Colander”
Lines 2, 3: January Gill O’Neil, “How to Love”
Line 4: January Gill O’Neil, “How to Love”
Line 5: Jacqueline Suskin, “Sunrise, Sunset”
Line 6: Jacqueline Suskin, “Sunrise, Sunset”
Line 7: Joshua Michael Stuart, “November Praise”
Line 8: Zeina Azzam, “Hugging the Tree”
Line 9: Zeina Azzam, “Hugging the Tree”
Line 10: Margaret Hasse, “With Trees”/Zeina Azzam, “Hugging the Tree”
Line 11: Stuart Kestenbaum, “Holding the Light”
Line 12: Stuart Kestenbaum, “Holding the Light”/Yvonne Zipter, “Seeds”

“For Today” is a tanka inspired by “Fado” by Jane Hirshfield from *The Beauty: Poems* (Knopf, 2017).

“In Search of Lost Birds” is inspired by a line from “A Lover From Palestine” by Mahmoud Darwish from *A Lover From Palestine and other Poems: An Anthology of Palestinian Poetry* (Palestine Information Office, 1970).

“One Word Prayer” is inspired by “Because the World is in Need of Mercy” by Mary Katherine Creel, which first appeared on her Substack Publication *a small spectacle,* June, 2025.

“Graft” is inspired by “The Grove” by Michael Kleber-Diggs from *Worldly Things* (Milkweed Editions, 2022).

“Making Room” is inspired by “To Softness” by Heather Swan from *A Kinship with Ash* (Terrapin Books, 2020).

“Afternoon” is a tanka inspired by “Afternoon in the House” by Jane Kenyon from *The Best Poems of Jane Kenyon* (Greywolf Press, 2020).

“Fist-Heart Turned Peony” is inspired by “Kindergarten Studies the Human Heart” by Diana Whitney from *Dark Beds (*June Road Press, 2023).

“It’s a Lot to Ask” is inspired by “Home in the Woods” by Linda Hogan from *Dark. Sweet.: New and Selected Poems* (Coffee House Press, 2014).

“What the Soil Knows” is inspired by “And What my Species Did” by Elizabeth Willis, published in *Harper’s Magazine,* April 2022.

“Archeology” is inspired by “Hibernal” by Babette Deutsch from *Honey out of the Rock* (B. Appleton, 1925).

“On a Winter Morning” is inspired by “A Winter Morning” by Ted Kooser from *Delights and Shadows* (Copper Canyon Press, 2004).

“Shaping a Soft Place” is inspired by “So Much Space for Song” by James Crews from *Turning Toward Grief: Reflections on Life, Loss & Appreciation* (Broadleaf Books, 2025).

“Such Love If You Let It” is inspired by “Wedding Poem” by Ross Gay from *Catalog of Unabashed Gratitude* (University of Pittsburgh Press, 2015).

“Dinner” is inspired by “The Suitor” by Jane Kenyon from *The Best Poems of Jane Kenyon* (Greywolf Press, 2020).

“Wider Than That” is a cento poem composed of lines by Mary Oliver. All poems from *Devotions* (Penguin Press, 2017). Note: several poems in the collection are entitled “Spring,” differentiated here by page number. Line credits as follows:

Title: “The World I Live in”
Line 1: “Spring” pg. 317
Lines 2, 3, 4: “Entering the Kingdom”
Line 5: “Spring” pg. 202
Line 6: “Spring” pg. 202/ “Spring” pg. 318
Line 7: “Spring” pg. 318

Line 8: “The Pond”
Lines 9, 10, 11: “Little Owl Who lives in the Orchard”
Line 12: “This Morning”
Lines 13,14: “Whistling Swans”
Line 15: “Little Owl Who Lives in the Orchard”
Line 16: “White Night”
Line 17: “The Night Traveler”
Line 18: “Logos”
Lines 19, 20: “The Night Traveler”

“Each time I finish a poem” borrows the last line adapted from the poem “Seasoning” by Jen Feroze, 2025.

“How You Know” is a tribute inspired by a poem of the same title by James Crews from *Turning Toward Grief: Reflections on Life, Loss & Appreciation* (Broadleaf Books, 2025).

About the Author

Ellen Rowland is a writer and editor who leads small, generative poetry workshops on craft and form. She is the author of three collections of haiku: *The Echo of Silence, Light Come Gather Me,* and *Blue Seasons,* as well as the book *Everything I Thought I Knew,* essays on living, learning, and parenting outside the status quo.

Her writing has appeared in numerous literary journals and in several poetry anthologies, most recently *The Path to Kindness* and *The Wonder of Small Things* edited by James Crews, and *Facing Goodbye* by The Wee Sparrow Poetry Press. Her debut collection of full-length poems, *No Small Thing,* was published by Fernwood Press in 2023. She is a Best of the Net nominee for her poem "When the World Was Whole." Ellen lives off the grid with her family on a small farm in Greece.

www.ingramcontent.com/pod-product-compliance
Lightning Source LLC
LaVergne TN
LVHW090618110826
845146LV00001B/439

* 9 7 9 8 9 0 1 4 6 7 1 7 6 *